Embark

~~~~~~~~~~~

A Six-Part Study
to Launch Your Group

ROBBY ANGLE

Cover & Interior Design by Outskirts Studio

Produced by **Trueface**
Trueface.org
ISBN: 978-1-7348805-6-4

Printed in the United States.

Contents

Getting Started

Welcome to *Embark!* This study is designed to help you launch your group. We believe that if you really dig into these exercises over the next six meetings, you will lay the foundation for a transformational group marked by authentic community and spiritual growth. You can find all the session videos and additional resources at *trueface.org/embark-group.* Simply sign up for a free account and choose the *Embark* course. You'll also find the **Group Map** here for you to print out and use as you work through this study.

Embark pairs with *The Cure for Groups*, Trueface's primary resource for group leaders. So, if you're this group's leader, make sure to grab a copy to unpack these concepts more. In both *The Cure for Groups* and *Embark*, we use the metaphor of a ship to help guide you along the five Core Components of a group, including:

The Destination:
Determine the Goals of Your Group

The Captain:
Lead with Intentionality and Vulnerability

The Crew:
Clarify Your Group Culture

The Ship:
Design Your Time for Transformation

The Route:
Plan Ahead to Get Where You Want to Go

Embark is structured similarly to other Trueface studies, which means that within each meeting we go through three sections:

Connect

We spend time connecting with each other in order to grow in our relationships.

Learn

We use content to help us learn and as a catalyst for growth.

Live

We discuss and apply what we learned to our actual lives, so that we can live out and experience these truths.

How to facilitate: This study has a higher degree of structure in order to work through some practical applications and set your group up well. We have provided recommended time frames to help you stay on track. Those time frames reference a sixty- or ninety-minute group meeting.

TRUEFACE

beyond the mask

Today's culture is perfecting the art and science of creating masks. Behind these masks, people are dying inside. **We're here to change that.**

Trueface equips people to experience the freedom of living beyond the mask, because behind the mask is the real you. When we increase trust in our relationships, we are able to experience being more authentically known and loved by God and others.

We hope to be a bridge for hundreds of thousands to experience the peace and freedom of the original good news by trusting God and others with their whole selves . . . the self behind the mask.

To learn more about Trueface, visit trueface.org, or join the thousands of people living the Trueface life on social media.

- Instagram: @truefacelife
- Facebook: @truefacecommunity
- Twitter: @truefaced

Trueface is a non-profit supported by people who have been impacted by the ministry. To partner with us in creating resources like the one you're about to experience, visit *trueface.org/give*.

Logistics

You'll find the videos and other additional resources for this study at *trueface.org/embark-group*. The videos and resources are free to use and are broken up by each meeting. Simply create a free account and sign up for the *Embark* course to get access to this content. Here you'll also find the **Group Map** for you to print out and use as you travel through this study.

Starting below is a place for you to write down what dates you'll be meeting, where you'll be meeting, and the most important thing—who'll be bringing the food! Fill out this section with your group members in your first meeting.

MEETING 1: SETTING SAIL

Celebrate the Start of Your Group

Date: _____

Location: _____

Snacks: _____

MEETING 2: THE DESTINATION

Determine the Goals of Your Group

Date: _____

Location: _____

Snacks: _____

MEETING 3: THE CAPTAIN, PART 1

Lead with Intentionality and Vulnerability

Date: _____

Location: _____

Snacks: _____

MEETING 4: THE CAPTAIN, PART 2

Lead with Intentionality and Vulnerability

Date: _____

Location: _____

Snacks: _____

MEETING 5: THE CREW AND THE SHIP

*Clarify Your Group Culture and Design Your
Time for Transformation*

Date: _____

Location: _____

Snacks: _____

MEETING 6: THE ROUTE

Plan Ahead to Get Where You Want to Go

Date: _____

Location: _____

Snacks: _____

EMBARK: A 6-PART STUDY TO LAUNCH YOUR GROUP

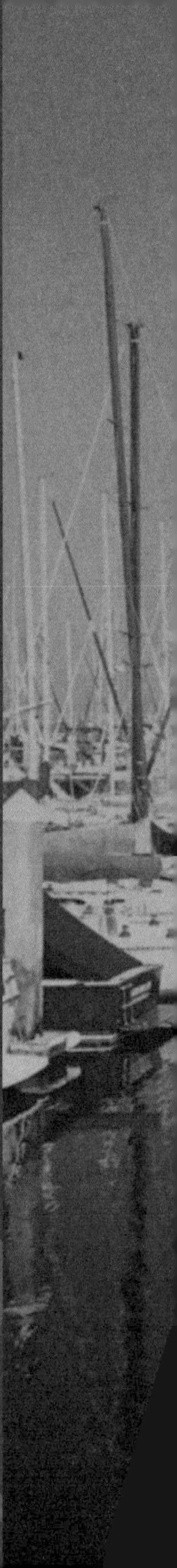

Setting Sail

CELEBRATE THE START OF YOUR GROUP

"They that go down to the sea in ships,
that do business in great waters;
These see the works of the Lord,
and his wonders in the deep."

PSALM 107:23-24

 **MEETING TOGETHER**

Connect

🕐 **THIS WILL TAKE ABOUT 10% OF YOUR TIME THIS WEEK (5-10 MINUTES BASED ON A 60-90 MINUTE MEETING)**

When everybody is welcomed and gathered, kick off the meeting by having someone from the group read the following out loud:

- "Welcome to *Embark*! Over the next six meetings, you are going to explore and discover what you want this group to be about spiritually, relationally, and logistically. We don't know about you, but we don't like when a group feels like an obligation or something to check off our list, and we definitely don't like walking away from meeting together thinking, "Was that a good use of my time?" Instead, we want to help you make this group an intentional and transformational part of your life—something you look forward to and prioritize because it's that worthwhile. As Psalm 107:23-24 says, we want to go see God's wonders in the deep together. This session will be a little different as we kick it off. Our main goal for tonight is to get to know each other and enjoy each other's company."

- Have someone pray to open this time, thanking God for the journey you're about to start together.

NOTES

Learn

🕐 10% OF YOUR TIME (10 MINUTES)

> ▷ **WATCH THE "SETTING SAIL" VIDEO**
> Find at *trueface.org/embark-group.*

Live

◐ 80% OF YOUR TIME (40-70 MINUTES)

Break up into pairs now and use the pages 13-15 for questions and notes.

INSTRUCTION REMINDER:

- Partner up, set a timer, and take turns asking questions to each other.

- Rotate partners after five minutes until you get a chance to talk with every other person.

- When you have had time with every person in the group, circle back up and have everybody share one thing that stood out about someone else in the group.

- Leave five to ten minutes for the leader to wrap up your time.

NOTES

LEADER WRAP UP // BEFORE YOU LEAVE:

- Pin down your next several meeting times, dates, and locations (use the Logistics Calendar on pages 5-6 if helpful).

- Print out a Group Map for each member at *trueface.org/embark-group* before your next meeting.

- Look at the next Diving Deeper section together to make sure no one has questions on what they should do before the next meeting. Reading the Diving Deeper section is not mandatory to engage in the group, but it will provide helpful context and processing time for you before heading into the next meeting.

- Clarify how you will share stories in Meetings 3 and 4.

 Tip: Try combining Meetings 3 & 4 into an overnighter for everyone to share stories. This is the best option, but we understand that planning can be difficult this early in a group.

- Pray to wrap up your time together.

QUESTION IDEAS:

The Basics:

- What's your name and do you like it?

- What does a typical weekend look like for you?

- Are you more of a cat, dog, bird, snake, chinchilla, or no-pet person?

- If you had to pick your ideal trip, would you rather it be relaxing or adventurous?

- What famous person would you want to have lunch with?

- Make up your own question: _____

  _____

A Little More Depth:

- What were you like in fourth grade?

- What is one thing that really brings you joy?

- When was the last time you felt really excited about something?

- When was the last time you felt really proud of something?

- Make up your own question: _____

  _____

NOTES

13

Deep Dives:

- What is one area in your life you would like to grow in?

- When you think about your parents or primary caregivers, what are the top three emotions that come up?

- What was one significant challenge you went through in high school?

- What is the bravest thing you've ever done?

- If you hit 90 years, what is something you want to be said about your life?

- Make up your own question: _____

_____

DIVING DEEPER
№ 01

The Destination: *Determine the Goals of Your Group*

These Diving Deeper sections are for your individual reflection between group meetings. They provide supplemental material and exercises to help you process and prepare for your next meeting in order to maximize your time. If you don't get to them, that's okay. Don't let it stop you from connecting with your community.

The Destination

Before you get on a ship—unless you're trying to skip town with a bunch of gold—you need to know where it's going, and you have to commit to the journey. Voyages are long. You don't want to embark on that kind of journey without knowing what the destination is. As Yogi Berra put it, "If you don't know where you're going, you'll end up someplace else."

This question of destination is foundational for any group that wants to grow together. Where do you want to go? Why are you going on this journey? Why did you write your name on that sign-up sheet, or agree to come to the first meeting? There may be several reasons. You may be wanting to grow relationally—make friends, be part of a community, spend time with other people that are on this journey. Maybe you want to see some changes in your life spiritually, emotionally, or practically, or maybe you just think being part of a group is something you're supposed to do, so you're following the script. If it's the last one, we hope to inspire you to dream a little bigger.

There are a ton of reasons you might be setting sail with this group, but the important thing is to clarify your destination with your group ahead of time. Often groups assume they have similar destinations in mind and don't realize there is a mismatch of expectations until they're drifting out in the middle of the ocean. We want your group to be intentional, transformational, and deeply worthwhile, and that means you need to know where you're going, and why! Use this Diving Deeper section to help you process your answers to these questions before your next group meeting. Then, when you all come together, you'll share some of your different "destinations" and decide where you want to go together.

DETERMINE YOUR DESTINATION:

- Why did you join this group? There is no wrong answer—this is a great time to be super honest with yourself.

Imagine yourself a year from now and answer the following questions.

- When I get to group, I feel:

NOTES

- Our relationships in this group are:
  Hint: Be specific! What are interactions like? What do you do together? How do you feel about the other group members?

- Spiritually, the biggest areas in which I've grown over the last year are:

- The group has helped me grow by:

REFLECTION TIME:

Take a few moments to reflect on this excerpt of a prayer from Sir Francis Drake, a famous explorer and navigator.

"Disturb us, Lord, to dare more boldly,
To venture on wider seas
Where storms will show your mastery;
Where losing sight of land,
We shall find the stars.

We ask You to push back
The horizons of our hopes;
And to push into the future
In strength, courage, hope, and love."

Pray some version of this prayer with us, and let the Holy Spirit respond by pausing to listen, reflect, or take notes.

God, I may know a lot of things that I want, but those aren't always what I need. What do I need in this season? Father, what do you hope for my heart in this coming season?

NOTES

EMBARK: A 6-PART STUDY TO LAUNCH YOUR GROUP

The Destination

DETERMINE THE GOALS OF YOUR GROUP

"If one does not know to which port one is sailing, no wind is favorable."

—LUCIUS ANNAEUS SENECA

MEETING TOGETHER

Read as a group: As you learned in your Diving Deeper section this week, determining why you're here and where you want to go is fundamental to having the kind of group you'll talk about for the rest of your life (in a good way). This week, you'll decide where you want to go together, because knowing where you're going helps you get there.

Connect

🕐 **THIS WILL TAKE ABOUT 30% OF YOUR TIME TODAY (15-30 MINUTES)**

NOTES

- Have someone kick off your time in prayer.

- Warm up questions:

  » What is the most fun trip you've ever been on? Why? (Quick stories!)

  » Why did you join this group? Remember, there are no wrong answers.

  » What are a few words that came to mind when you thought about what you want this group to look like in a year? Have you experienced this somewhere else?

Learn

 10% OF YOUR TIME (10 MINUTES)

 WATCH "THE DESTINATION" VIDEO
Find at *trueface.org/embark-group.*

Live

 60% OF YOUR TIME (35-50 MINUTES)

Now you get to try it out and determine your destination! Creating and clarifying your group goals will help you head in the direction you actually want to go. The purpose of this Live section is to make these Core Components practical and applicable, so below we guide you through a group exercise to create these goals.

You can take notes here in this book, on a big flip chart, a white board, a shared digital note, or anything else that works for your group. Regardless of your method, have someone take notes for the whole group so that you stay on the same page. We've also provided a space for you on page 30 to take group notes.

> *Tip: It is helpful to have sticky notes for everyone to write down various thoughts and comments and then hand them to the facilitator to organize them on a wall or table.*

NOTES

- **Relationships Reflection:** *(5 minutes)* Start by giving everybody a couple minutes to jot down their thoughts on the relationship questions below.

  » What do we want our relationships to be like a year from now?

  » How would we know that this was true? In other words, what would this look like?

- **Group Sharing:** *(5-10 minutes)* Share as a group and have the note taker organize the comments shared. Just get all your thoughts out on the table for now.

- **Spiritual Growth Reflection:** *(5 minutes)* Give everyone a few minutes to write down some thoughts on spiritual growth goals.

  » How do we hope our relationship with God changes in this next year?

» How do we want to grow or mature in our faith?

» How would we know that this was true? What would this look like?

- **Group Sharing:** *(5-10 minutes)* Share as a group with the note taker organizing the comments shared.

- **Group Discussion:** *(5-10 minutes)* Develop your group goals.

  » Look at your notes for Relationships Reflection. What similarities do you see? Can any be combined?

  » If you need to pair them down more, have everyone vote for the top three they're most excited about. You can vote by raising hands, passing in post-it notes, or however else works for your group. Remember, be true to what you really think!

NOTES

» If you still have too many different ideas on the table, take away the ones that got the fewest votes, and vote again until you have just a few that everyone's on board with.

» Try to put these into one statement that captures your Relationship goal. For example, "Our goal is to have real relationships where we live life together." Remember, your group goals should help clarify the collective hopes and expectations of the group. They should clarify why you are meeting in order to clarify the destination that you collectively hope to arrive at as a group.

» Repeat this for the Spiritual Growth ideas to pair them down and create a goal statement for this area.

 Tip: Remember, 80% is a win! Don't overthink it. Someone in the room might want to make these perfect. That's not the point. Do they capture the essence of the relational and spiritual goals for the group? That is the goal.

- **Group Discussion:** *(5 minutes)* Process the following questions as a group.

  » Does it feel like anything's missing regarding the hopes and goals that we discussed tonight?

  » Are our goals important enough to us to prioritize this group despite the busyness of life?

LEADER WRAP UP // BEFORE YOU LEAVE:

- Write down your Destination on your Group Map (remember, you can find this at *trueface.org/ embark-group*).

- Confirm who will be sharing stories along with the leader during the next meeting.

- Look at the next Diving Deeper section together to help you prepare for the next two meetings where everyone will be sharing stories.

- Confirm your next meeting time and date.

- Pray to wrap up your time together.

NOTES

RELATIONSHIPS NOTES	SPIRITUAL GROWTH NOTES

OUR GROUP GOALS

DIVING DEEPER

Nº 02

The Captain: *Lead with Intentionality and Vulnerability, Part 1*

These Diving Deeper sections are for your individual reflection between group meetings. They provide supplemental material and exercises to help you process and prepare for your next meeting in order to maximize your time. If you don't get to them, that's okay. Don't let it stop you from connecting with your community.

The Captain
PART 1

In *The Cure for Groups* we share about why a leader's choice to be vulnerable is so influential—the crew of a ship looks to their captain for signals on what they should be doing or what kind of team they are going to be. If the captain is content to just hang out close to the shoreline, the crew will probably stick to the shallows as well. If, however, the captain is willing to strike out into deeper waters, the crew has a much better chance of heading there too.

While we do believe that the leader is very influential in setting the tone for a group, each and every member also sets an example and signals what they want the group to feel like. Do you step in or withdraw? Are you authentic or veiled? Do you choose vulnerability or safety?

Vulnerability is the bedrock of a truly transformational, powerful, I-can't-wait-to-go group. You don't have to choose it—you can keep it light and shallow, but you'll probably be bored and wonder if you should have gotten some errands done instead.

Increasing our ability to be vulnerable is not easy, because it is connected to core fears and beliefs about our identity. In order to risk vulnerability, we need to understand that *who we are is more important than what we do.* If our identity is secure, then we are able to take risks of being vulnerable because our identity

NOTES

is determined by who God says we are, and not the view or affirmations of others. When we stand secure in our identity as God's adopted sons and daughters, we let others know our strengths and our weaknesses without the fear of rejection or the need of approval.

Vulnerability gives others the opportunity to love the real you, instead of the person you might pretend to be. In our relationship with God and our relationships with others, we have to trust that our true heart and person is more valued than our actions or behaviors— good or bad.

We want to quickly clarify what we mean by vulnerability. Vulnerability is not transparency. Transparency shares information but keeps people at arm's length, like letting someone look in the windows of your house. Vulnerability seeks connection, inviting them to come inside and see the beautiful staircase and messy bathrooms. When we are vulnerable, we let people sit with us in our pain, rather than just telling them about it. Further, when we are vulnerable about our hopes and dreams, we invite others in to celebrate alongside us.

We'll be honest—this kind of vulnerability does carry the possibility of being hurt. As a friend of ours says, it's like "giving bullets" to someone that they can use to either protect you or hurt you. Vulnerability takes courage. But the freedom you experience by being fully known is amazing, and that freedom is attractive and infectious. Vulnerability is the secret sauce for the kind of group you talk about the rest of your life.

NOTES

Vulnerability and trust go hand in hand, and trust is built, not assumed. You have to risk some vulnerability to build some trust and vice versa. This week, try to risk some vulnerability in order to build more trust in your group by sharing your story, asking the Holy Spirit to guide you as you process what you're ready to share.

PREPARING TO SHARE YOUR STORY:

Telling our story isn't always the most straightforward thing, so we want to help you prepare. First, we'll help you process your story for yourself. Then, we'll help you process how to share with the group.

For You

On the following two pages use the **Life Map** and four questions to help you unpack your story.

Life Map: Plot the high points (+10s) on the right and low points (-10s) on the left chronologically. You can also print out another map at *trueface.org/embark-group* if you need more space.

LIFE MAP

BIRTH

TODAY

Questions: Take notes with what comes to mind regarding the following questions.

What are three words that described your home growing up?	Who has been an influential person in your life and why?
If you didn't incorporate your faith story into the timeline, write it out here.	In this next season, what do you think God wants for your heart and for your relationship with Him?

SHARING WITH THE GROUP:

You don't need to share everything from the previous exercise with your group—in fact, if you did, it would probably take a few hours! Over time, many of these events and experiences will come up on their own if your group is committed to living vulnerably.

To prepare for sharing your story, look back at your Life Map and circle six events that you feel were particularly influential and that you are willing to share. Remember, you will signal how vulnerable and authentic you want this group to be. Is there something on your Life Map that makes your heart beat a little faster when you think about sharing it? Or is there something you didn't include on your Life Map because you prefer to keep it hidden? Consider sharing this uncomfortable topic. It takes a lot of courage, and it's alright if you're not ready. Talk to God about it, and ask yourself some questions like, "Why am I so worried about sharing this? What am I afraid it will say about me?"

Use the template on the next page to guide your story and help you incorporate your answers from the 4 questions on page 38.

NOTES

STORY TEMPLATE:

I'm _____ .

I grew up in _____ and three

words that described my home growing up were:

_____, _____, and

_____.

6 Life Events (include pieces of your faith journey).

- •

- •

- •

- •

- •

- •

The person that was the most influential to me was

_____, because . . .

In this next season, what I think God wants for my

heart and my relationship with Him is . . .

NOTES

REFLECTION TIME:

Pray some version of this prayer with us, and let the Holy Spirit respond.

God, show me my life journey through Your eyes. Help me to see how You've been weaving a masterful story together, unique to me and my heart. Guide me as I decide what to share with this group and remind me that Your courageous Spirit lives in me.

NOTES

The Captain

LEAD WITH INTENTIONALITY AND VULNERABILITY

PART 1

First of Two Weeks Sharing Stories

*"We cannot lead anyone farther than
we have been ourselves."*

—JOHN C. MAXWELL

MEETING TOGETHER

Read as a group: If you want a transformational and meaningful group, you need to be willing to wade into deeper waters. This is leadership. Most groups have someone in the role of facilitator or group leader, but each of you also have the opportunity to lead by the example you set in sharing with vulnerability. It's far easier to keep things light and surface level, but this doesn't lead to the kind of relationships and spiritual growth that we were made for—the kind where you know that who you are is more important than what you do. By sharing your story, you invite the other people in your group to know and love the real you and build a foundation for meaningful, authentic relationships.

This week and next week will focus on sharing stories. The members that don't share in this meeting will share in the next meeting. There are many ways to share your stories. Use this as a guide, not a formula. In other words, do what fits your group the best.

Connect

🕐 10% OF YOUR TIME

- Have someone open in prayer.

- Warm up question:

  » What is a personal high or a low from this past week?

NOTES

- For those of you that are sharing this meeting:

  » Have you shared your story before?

  » How are you feeling about telling your story? Are there any fears about it that you're comfortable sharing with the group?

Learn
🕐 **10% OF YOUR TIME**

▷ **WATCH "THE CAPTAIN - PART 1" VIDEO**
Find at *trueface.org/embark-group.*

Live
◐ **80% OF YOUR TIME**

Now is when the rubber meets the road—or perhaps the wind hits the sails. Talking and learning about vulnerability is wonderful, but it begins to transform our lives and relationships when we practice it and live it out. Try practicing vulnerability and courage as you share your stories with each other.

OUR CAPTAIN AGREEMENT:

Pull out your Group Map and review the Captain Agreement, or visit *trueface.org/embark-group* if you haven't printed it out yet. Take a few minutes to individually reflect on if you're willing to make this

NOTES

commitment. If you are, initial the agreement. If you aren't, that's okay. We hope that through time and built trust, you will feel comfortable committing to this with your group. Then, starting with the leader, begin sharing your stories.

THINGS TO KEEP IN MIND:

- Have a clock to help whoever is sharing stay on track. Set the timer to ten minutes and have someone let the person sharing know when they have two minutes left.

- After each person finishes, leave about five minutes for questions or extra sharing time. Good questions are ones that help you understand the person and their experience more deeply.

- When someone else is sharing, listen to understand. Try to really hear their experience. If you haven't shared yet, it can be easy to spend your time worrying about sharing your own story, rather than listening to whoever's sharing in the moment. Try to set that aside and enter into their story.

- Resist the urge to problem solve or correct anyone while they tell their story.

- Allow people to experience their emotions. It's okay if they feel sad, angry, or distressed at different points in their story.

- Always feel free to pray for someone if they are in a position of particular need.

- Take notes in the following pages for things you want to remember from the stories shared.

LEADER WRAP UP // BEFORE YOU LEAVE:

- Remind those that didn't share during this meeting that they'll be sharing next meeting.

- Confirm your next meeting time and date.

- Pray to wrap up your time together.

NOTES

DIVING DEEPER

№ 03

The Captain: *Lead with Intentionality and Vulnerability, Part 2*

These Diving Deeper sections are for your individual reflection between group meetings. They provide supplemental material and exercises to help you process and prepare for your next meeting in order to maximize your time. If you don't get to them, that's okay. Don't let it stop you from connecting with your community.

The Captain
PART 2

The desire to be fully known and loved is in our bones. God designed us to grow spiritually by connecting relationally. Put another way, real, authentic relationships are vital to our spiritual growth. We innately have a deep longing for these kinds of relationships, to live in that space beyond the mask where our shame and insecurities take a back seat. We want to experience the freedom, peace, and joy of deep relationships with others—we were made for it.

If we are made for these kinds of life-altering relationships, and if Jesus modeled them for us, then why do so few of us experience them? Why do they seem so difficult to find or cultivate or keep?

There are three levels that describe our relationships. Most of us get dead-scared at around level two and rarely experience the love, freedom, and growth that accompanies level three. Level three is where the gold is. It is where we experience deep connections that are critical in helping us mature in our relationship with God.

LEVEL ONE

This is the acquaintance level. We make social connections with people who enjoy the same things as us or have the same hobbies. Maybe our kids play together. We might be on the same project at work or in the same running club. These relationships are convenient and meet a need we have. We share surface-level things and thrive on small nuggets of truth about ourselves. With enough time, these small nuggets slowly build up, creating little blocks of trust that can eventually lead to level two.

LEVEL TWO

This is the friendship level. As friends, we invite each other to come closer, to see a little more of us. We hang out in this space for a while, because there are lots of safe things to share and trust others with. Level two is a great stage where we each benefit from and enjoy the relationship. However, at the core, friendships are still primarily about us. This smaller group of our friends help us have fun, feel loved, and feel connected. Most of us experience this level of relationship and rarely venture past it.

We get stuck here ... because we're afraid.

There's a tension between the second and third levels called shame. It tells us that this person is our friend now while they know the easier, safer parts of us, but if we let them into the darker rooms of our hearts they'll reject us.

So, we stay at level two, hiding the things we're ashamed of and wondering why we still don't feel that deep connection we long for. We trust more than we did at level one, but there are still a lot of caveats. Level two is just too comfortable to leave, but when we stay there, we miss out on what level three has to offer—and what we really desire.

LEVEL THREE

This is the level of deep friendship. It's a place where the best and worst of you can be known by the other person. It's a place where the other person knows your ugly stories and they don't move an inch. It's a place where you don't have any more, "Well, I don't know if they'd accept me if they knew that." Level three relationships are where you feel fully known and fully loved, where love truly casts out fear because you've trusted each other.

Level three relationships are more about the other person than about us. It is where we protect each other's weaknesses and submit to each other's strengths, being healthier and stronger through those relationships than we are without them. These relationships are consistent and intentional. A level three relationship usually takes time and a conversation to speak to the importance and priority of the relationship.

We want your group to move through these three levels. This takes time and risk and a lot of built-up trust, but like we said before—level three is where the gold is.

REFLECTION QUESTIONS:

Do you have any friends you feel like are level three friends? What makes them level three friends?

Is there anyone in level two that you feel like you could trust enough to venture into level three? When you consider it, what emotions or thoughts come up for you?

What keeps you from going to level three with people? Do you resonate with the barrier of shame, or is it a different barrier for you?

NOTES

What's something someone shared last meeting that felt like a "level three" share? How can you reach out to them and affirm them?

If you haven't shared your story yet, see Diving Deeper 2 to help you prepare.

NOTES

REFLECTION TIME:

Pray some version of this prayer with us, and let the Holy Spirit respond.

God, sometimes it's hard for me to believe that you died not only for my sin, but for my shame. Help me to receive Your grace and help me to believe that You fully know and fully love me. Teach me to trust the way You see me, instead of how I see me, and then teach me to trust others with the real me.

NOTES

EMBARK: A 6-PART STUDY TO LAUNCH YOUR GROUP

The Captain

LEAD WITH INTENTIONALITY AND VULNERABILITY

PART 2

Second Week of Sharing Stories

"Vulnerability is not weakness; it's our greatest measure of courage."

—BRENÉ BROWN

MEETING TOGETHER

Read as a group: This week we will continue to share stories. Our stories provide insights into the unique design and journey God has given us. Let's jump straight in and continue with our stories to make sure everyone gets to share.

Connect
⏱ **10% OF YOUR TIME**

- Have someone open in prayer.

- For those of you that are sharing this meeting:

  » Have you shared your story before?

  » How are you feeling about telling your story? Are there any fears about it that you're comfortable sharing with the group?

Learn
⏱ **10% OF YOUR TIME**

WATCH "THE CAPTAIN - PART 2" VIDEO
Find at *trueface.org/embark-group.*

Live

🕐 **80% OF YOUR TIME**

Remember: Now is when the rubber meets the road—
or perhaps the wind hits the sails. Talking and learning
about vulnerability and authenticity is wonderful,
but it is in practicing and living it out that it begins
to transform our lives and relationships. Practice
vulnerability and courage as you share your stories
with each other.

Review the "Things to Keep in Mind" on page 46,
and jump in.

After everyone has gone, invite those that are
comfortable to share what it was like to tell their
story. Sometimes sharing vulnerable stories can feel
relieving or anxiety-provoking or leave us wondering
what others are thinking. So, if you are comfortable,
share what telling your story was like for you.

> 💡 *Tip: Look for ways to affirm each other's stories.*

LEADER WRAP UP // BEFORE YOU LEAVE:

- Look at the next Diving Deeper section together
  to make sure everyone knows what they need to
  process before next meeting.

- Confirm your next meeting time and date.

- Pray to wrap up your time together.

DIVING DEEPER

№ 04

The Crew and The Ship: Clarify Your Group Culture and Design Your Time for Transformation

These Diving Deeper sections are for your individual reflection between group meetings. They provide supplemental material and exercises to help you process and prepare for your next meeting in order to maximize your time. If you don't get to them, that's okay. Don't let it stop you from connecting with your community.

The Crew

You can have a great destination chosen and a wonderful captain, but if you have a mistrusting, conflict-prone crew your chances of a successful voyage are pretty slim. If no one is sure what their role is, what the expectations are, or how they're supposed to interact with each other, then every task is going to feel like an uphill battle instead of a smooth, coordinated operation. You'll spend more time mediating tense interactions than sailing. Establishing your crew's culture is vital.

Have you ever been in a group where things went sideways? Where one member shared something sensitive with someone outside the group? Ever had things get tense in the middle of a meeting, where someone essentially shames another for an honest question or struggle? Or how about when there are unwritten rules about how certain people interact, like, "Everyone knows you don't question him if he says it in that tone," or, "Once she gets going, she just plows on for twenty minutes," or, "If someone says something uncomfortable, we just move on."

Every group of humans—whether it's a family, church group, or work team—has a culture. These microcultures come with spoken and unspoken rules of how we all interact and what's expected of us. Think of your family growing up. Most likely there were unspoken expectations about how you functioned, who was allowed to be questioned or not, what you did in conflict, and how you expressed yourself to others. These culture-creating phenomena aren't inherently good or bad. One of the biggest factors determining whether a culture is healthy or harmful is whether it was created intentionally and with clear expectations. So, this week we will reflect on the kinds of values you want to describe your group culture and explore what commitments you can make together to protect those values.

The Ship

In addition to the culture of the crew, the design of the ship itself is hugely important for a voyage. Ships are designed for specific purposes. A week aboard a tugboat would be a lousy way to spend a trip to the Virgin Islands. Likewise, a sailing catamaran would never be able to push a three-hundred-ton barge through the currents of the Mississippi. The design of the ship deeply affects how the captain and crew spend their time on this adventure. While the destination may be exciting, the ship is where you actually live on your way there.

Believe it or not, meeting together for 60 or 90 minutes once a week is not in and of itself a recipe for spiritual growth or authentic relationships. How you spend your time together is what carries you toward your destination, and that structure can either help or hinder your progress.

NOTES

There are three aspects to how you spend your time: connecting, learning, and living it out. Connecting relationally builds the foundation for vulnerability and genuine community. We then engage in learning together as a catalyst for growth. Finally, we talk about how to put what we're learning into practice in our real, everyday lives.

Unfortunately, this aspect of applying what we're learning has been used as a weapon against many of us. We may have experienced this being a way to "keep us in line" or check up on us, or as a way to prove how good of a Christian we were. This isn't what we mean at all. When we try to apply truth in a genuine, safe group, we get to help each other discover more ways to let the grace and power of Jesus pour into our daily lives. It's about letting God do more in our lives—not trying to prove how much we can do for God.

In this Diving Deeper, we want to help you think through what kind of culture you want to build and what commitments you think will help you stay there. We'll also help you think through how you intentionally spend your time in your group. We want to use our time purposefully in all areas of life.

THE CREW:

Clarify Your Group Culture

Use the questions and lists below to reflect on what kind of culture you want to build in your group.

- What makes a group feel safe to you? What makes a group feel unsafe to you?

- Have you experienced an unhealthy culture, either in another group, in your family, in a sports team, or at work? What were the unwritten rules or expectations of that culture?

- What do you want to define your culture? Look at the list below for ideas and add any others that you think of. Circle your top ten and put a checkmark next to your top five.

Our Group's Culture Is . . .

Fun	Tight knit	Casual
Safe	Vulnerable	Formal
Authentic	Daring	Spontaneous
Powerful	Sensitive	Timely
Brave	Caring	Purposeful
Silly	Wise	Emotional
Thoughtful	Deep	Flexible
Joyful	Transparent	Real
Intellectual	Funny	Open
Challenging	Focused	Comfortable
Welcoming	Serious	Easy-going

- What are some commitments that you think would help protect this kind of culture? Look at the list on the following page for ideas and write in your own. Circle your top ten, and then put a checkmark next to your top three.

To Protect and Create This Culture . . .

We don't fix.

We stand with each other.

We commit to confidentiality.

We don't preach.

We don't demean.

We wait to be asked before giving advice.

We practice radical candor.

We look for ways to affirm each other.

We don't do sarcasm.

We don't judge.

We don't take ourselves too seriously.

We look for ways to serve those around us.

We don't veer from scripture.

We listen first to understand.

We value who someone is over what they do.

We don't ignore conflict.

We prioritize listening to the Holy Spirit.

We have fun without negativity.

We believe _____.

We want to learn and grow.

We speak encouraging words.

We pray for each other weekly.

We serve together once per year, quarter, month, etc.

We memorize scripture.

NOTES

THE SHIP:

Design Your Time for Transformation

Consider the following questions as you process how your group is spending their time together.

How have other groups (or this group) spent their time together? Write out a general schedule below (for example, "30 minutes socializing, 15 minutes of highs/lows, 20 minutes reading a Bible passage . . . ").

How do you feel about how you are spending your time? Is there any area that feels like you are either spending too much time or not enough?

Is there anything missing from your time together that you wish was part of the recipe?

REFLECTION TIME:

Pray some version of this prayer with us, and let the Holy Spirit respond.

God, I want to help build a culture that reflects You. Help me to see the ways I need to grow in loving others the way You do. Help me to pour Your love over the places I've been hurt.

The Crew and The Ship

CLARIFY YOUR GROUP CULTURE AND DESIGN YOUR TIME FOR TRANSFORMATION

"The alternative to good design is always bad design. There is no such thing as no design."

—ADAM JUDGE

MEETING TOGETHER

Read as a group: Our time together matters, both in how we interact and how we actually spend our time. Our family systems, organizations, churches, and friend groups all function with a set of spoken and unspoken rules or expectations, creating a unique culture for each group. If we don't intentionally create a culture we want, the culture will create itself with these unspoken rules baked right in.

Similarly, if we don't intentionally decide how we will spend our time in our group, we may find ourselves spending a lot of time together but not moving in the direction we actually want. We will drift along with the currents instead of purposefully sailing toward our destination.

Connect

 30% OF YOUR TIME

- Have someone open in prayer.

- Warm up questions:

    » What did rules look like in your home growing up? Spoken? Unspoken? Strict? Lax? Enforced by one parent or caregiver? Different for your siblings?

» What aspect of your life do you feel you're most intentional with? Least intentional? For example, your friendships, your health, your work, your kids, etc.

Learn
🕐 **10% OF YOUR TIME**

 WATCH "THE CREW AND THE SHIP" VIDEO
Find at *trueface.org/embark-group.*

Live
◐ **60% OF YOUR TIME**

NOTES

CREATE YOUR CULTURE:

We often don't intentionally create our cultures— instead they seem to just take form on their own. Unfortunately, this usually doesn't lead to a healthy culture. Use the following exercise to choose your values and commitments as a group, similarly to how you chose your destination in Week 2.

Values Reflection: *(5 minutes)* Reflect individually on the following questions and take notes on the values you hope this group embodies. Feel free to look back at page 74 from last week's Diving Deeper for a list of values.

- What qualities do we want to define the culture of this group? Put another way, how do we want to treat each other?

- Consider a really healthy culture you've experienced. What made it that way?

- What are your top five words you hope will describe the values of your group?

NOTES

Share Together: *(5-10 minutes)*

- Share your top five words as a group with a note taker organizing the comments shared. Have everyone give a short description of why they chose the values that they did.

- Once everyone has shared, see if there are any that could be combined together.

- Everyone gets three votes for their top choices. Remember everyone, be true to what you really think!

- Depending on how much agreement you have, you might only need to vote once. However, you may need to keep eliminating some and then vote again. Repeat until you have between three and five values that everyone feels excited about. Write them below.

NOTES

Commitments Reflection: *(5 minutes)* Take five minutes to reflect individually on the following question. Feel free to look back at page 75 from last week's Diving Deeper for some starting points for commitments.

- What commitments could we make that will help protect the culture we want to have?

Share Together: *(5-10 minutes)*

- Just like with the values section, spend five to ten minutes sharing your commitment ideas as a group and make sure to describe what you mean by the commitments you share.

- Once everyone has shared, see if there are any that could be combined together.

- Again, have everyone give three votes for their top commitment choices.

- Repeat until you have three to five commitments that everyone feels excited about and write them below. Remember, less is more!

OUR CULTURE:

Our values are:

We commit to:

Design Your Time for Transformation: *(10-15 minutes)*

Just like how unintentional cultures don't usually end up healthy, unintentional time rarely gets us where we want to go. Use the following questions to help process how you're spending your time in the group.

- What are some great things about how we've been spending our time?

- What are some areas where we could be spending our time better?

- How will we incorporate the practice of asking "What faith step is God inviting me to take" to help us embed what we're learning into our real lives?

Use the pie chart on the following page to estimate how you want to spend your time in group.

 Tip: It may be helpful to think about this in terms of connect, learn, and live, and how your group wants to use its time for those three areas.

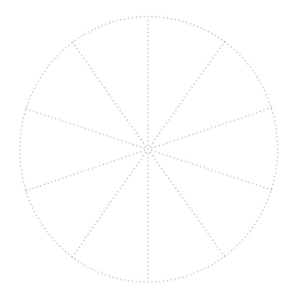

LEADER WRAP UP // BEFORE YOU LEAVE:

- Record your Crew Culture and your Ship Design on your Group Map. This map will help you remember the values and commitments you want to define this group and how you want to spend your time together.

- Look at the next Diving Deeper section together to help you prepare for your Route-Planning Session next meeting.

- Confirm your next meeting time and date.

- Pray to wrap up your time together.

DIVING DEEPER
№ 05

The Route: *Plan Ahead to Get Where You Want to Go.*

These Diving Deeper sections are for your individual reflection between group meetings. They provide supplemental material and exercises to help you process and prepare for your next meeting in order to maximize your time. If you don't get to them, that's okay. Don't let it stop you from connecting with your community.

The Route

One of the most critical responsibilities in sailing is navigating the route. The navigator has all kinds of information at their disposal: depth, tidal patterns, local and global wind patterns, weather forecasts, wave heights, currents, and hazards. It's a constant process of zooming out to see the big picture and then zooming in to make sure all is well in your immediate vicinity. You need to know the route you intend to take, and then consistently check in to make sure your ship is in line with that.

Groups are no different. They need to choose and navigate a route. Have you ever been in a group where every few weeks you're having the "what should we study next" conversation? This is like only looking at the two miles around your ship. It might keep you off of the rocks, but you have little chance of reaching your destination.

Planning ahead for where you want your group to go is vital for having a transformational group. Not only does this take the pressure off trying to figure this out after every study, but it also gives you a vision for what's coming and how it all fits together. Plus, instead of just showing up and seeing what the leader feels like studying, you get to be an integral part in deciding what you need and how to get there. You'll have skin in the game.

NOTES

If you plan your route ahead of time (we suggest four to six months at a time), you can also look ahead for busy seasons, like holidays, the end of the school year, or upcoming trips. Your calendar reflects your priorities, and planning ahead can help keep your group an integrated piece of your life rather than something you're trying to fit in. Additionally, one of the key ingredients that leads to transformational, incredible groups is going on a weekend retreat together—and that definitely requires planning ahead.

Below we'll help you think through what you want to study and experience with your group, so that when you come together, you will have a Route-Planning Session that Magellan would have been jealous of.

- What are some areas you'd like to learn more about? Have you been curious about the kings in the Old Testament? What about the real difference between joy and happiness? Something else?

- What are some areas of your life you would like to grow in? Patience, resilience, peace, rhythms of rest, trust, courage? Spend some time asking your Father to show you areas He wants to help you mature in.

NOTES

- What would be a meaningful way that you could serve with your group? Is there a population or issue that is close to your heart (even if you aren't sure how to serve yet)?

- What is a fun group activity? Game nights, holiday parties, paintball? Part of keeping connected with our groups is having fun together.

- Look at the next 6 months. What seasons do you see coming up that might impact your group's route? For example, some groups do shorter studies in the summer because many people are in and out of town, or they choose a particular study to go along with Easter. If you look ahead to page 103, we've provided a blank calendar for your group to fill out, and you can write some of these down there. Alternatively, you can print out calendars at *trueface.org/embark-group* for free.

Below are some examples of types of studies and activities you might choose. Circle the ones you're interested in.

Study Topics:

Peace	Holy Spirit	New Testament
Patience	Word Studies	Gospels
Sin	Marriage	Proverbs
Wisdom	Parenting	Psalms
Obedience	Dating	Apologetics
Joy	Friendships	Destiny
Rest	Vocation	Gifts of the Spirit
Solitude	Finances	Historical Context
Humility	Shame	Spiritual Rhythms
Service	Old Testament	Sin Cycles

Activities:

Game Night	Cultural Event	Pool Day
Movie Night	Sports Event	Bike Ride
Birthday Parties	Playing a Sport	Firepit Night
Holiday Parties	Hiking	Group Dinner
Local Festivals	Bowling	Playing Music
Camping	Cooking Night	Park Day
Concert	BBQ Cook-Out	Group Overnight

Service Opportunities and Populations:

Food Pantry

Foster Kids

Homeless Services

Soup Kitchen

Widow and Widower Ministries

Elderly

Elementary Schools

Middle Schools

High Schools

Other Religions

Other Ethnicities

Prisons

Teaching Skills to At-Risk Teens

Housing Help (Building, Fixing)

Juvenile Detention Centers

Mental Health Organizations

Addiction Centers

Local Neighborhood

Single Moms

Single Dads

Lower Socioeconomic Status

Adoption Centers

Crisis Pregnancy Centers

Community Resource Centers

EMBARK: A 6-PART STUDY TO LAUNCH YOUR GROUP

The Route

PLAN AHEAD FOR DEEPER CONNECTION

"To reach a port we must sail, sometimes with the wind, and sometimes against it. But we must not drift or lie at anchor."

—OLIVER WENDELL HOLMES

MEETING TOGETHER

Read as a group: In Week 2 we talked about how knowing where you're going helps you get there. Now is the time to really get into the nuts and bolts of how you're getting there—the route you're taking this ship on to get to your destination. This means looking not only at what kind of studies or curriculums you want to go through, but also deciding how you'll pursue connection, relationships, service, and whatever else your group has chosen as a priority.

Connect

 **30% OF YOUR TIME**

- Open in prayer.

- Warm up questions:

    » What is something you've learned about yourself in the last sixty days?

    » What is a personal area of growth you hope to experience in the next six months?

Learn

 10% OF YOUR TIME

 WATCH "THE ROUTE" VIDEO
Find at *trueface.org/embark-group.*

Live

60% OF YOUR TIME

It's not easy to plan ahead, and it's even harder to stick to it! Below we've included a calendar for you to brainstorm and choose your next four to six months together. Before you hammer out the details though, get everyone's thoughts out on the table with the following questions. Refer to pages 93 and 94 for ideas.

- What are a few areas you would like to learn more about?

- What are a few areas you would like to grow in?

NOTES

- What is an area of serving that you feel particularly drawn to? While we all can and should serve on our own, there is a uniquely powerful element to doing it together.

- What are a couple fun social activities you would like to do as a group?

 Tip: We strongly recommend doing an overnight retreat together twice a year. Time and again, we've seen this be a key element in the kind of group people talk about for the rest of their lives. Is this something your group is interested in? How could you make it happen?

Narrow the Focus: Start looking for similarities in everyone's answers. Use the calendar on page 102 or print out extras from *trueface.org/embark-group* and start actually putting things on your calendar. Remember, your calendar reflects your priorities, so if you haven't written it down, the odds of it really happening aren't good.

LAST AND CRITICAL STEP:

Put another "Route-Planning Session" on the calendar. This is a time to re-evaluate goals, check in on how everybody is doing, and do the same process of thinking through the next season's calendar and content plan. See the Route-Planning Meeting Guide on page 109 to use in future meetings.

NOTES

SUN	MON	TUES	WED	THUR	FRI	SAT

SUN	MON	TUES	WED	THUR	FRI	SAT

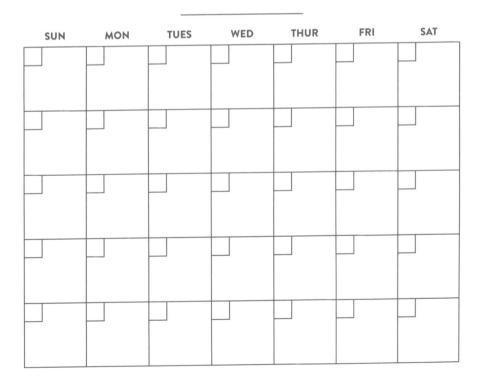

SUN	MON	TUES	WED	THUR	FRI	SAT

SUN	MON	TUES	WED	THUR	FRI	SAT

SUN	MON	TUES	WED	THUR	FRI	SAT

SUN	MON	TUES	WED	THUR	FRI	SAT

LEADER WRAP UP // BEFORE YOU LEAVE:

- Take a moment to celebrate the last six weeks. Your group has moved through some difficult waters together!

- Record your Route on your Group Map. This map will help you remember each of the Core Components of your group.

- Make sure you're all clear on what your next study is and the logistical steps for starting it. (Do books need to be ordered? Is someone else leading the first week?)

- Confirm your next meeting time and date.

- Pray to wrap up your time together.

NOTES

BON VOYAGE!

God designed us to live in real, authentic relationships. They are how we grow and mature. They're also one of the primary ways God infuses joy and meaning and life into us. So, dive in! Your group can be the kind that you talk about for the rest of your life. Don't settle for mediocre relationships and boring gatherings. Hoist the sails, throw off the bowlines! Be brave, trust God's Spirit, and set sail into the wild waters of life-giving groups.

"Twenty years from now you will be more disappointed by the things you didn't do than by the ones you did do. So, throw off the bowlines! Sail away from safe harbor. Catch the trade winds in your sails. Explore. Dream. Discover!"

—MARK TWAIN

Route-Planning Session

SEASONAL CHECK-IN MEETING GUIDE

"You've got to think about 'big things' while you're doing small things, so that all the small things go in the right direction."

—ALVIN TOFFLER

Diving Deeper to Prepare for Your Seasonal Route-Planning Session:

There are rhythms and cycles that God has given us that lead to blessing and clarity. God has given us a weekly rhythm that includes a day of rest. He has given us four seasons which lead to annual cycles for growth and renewal. There is a cycle to the day for waking and sleeping, working and resting. Further, there are seasons of relationships. We have seasons of being in new relationships with heightened emotions and mature relationships filled with steadiness and depth. Many of us will experience the cycle of our children maturing, and we may even see the cycle start again with grandkids.

Rhythms and cycles are good. Relationships mature and grow. Groups are the same. All groups, just like all teams, change and grow for a myriad of reasons. One of the greatest challenges in groups is knowing how to navigate the changing group dynamic over the months and years. Some groups should wrap up and transition after six months. Some should stay together for forty years. How do you know the wisest thing for your group?

Trust the Spirit. Ask God for clarity. What's best and wisest isn't necessarily the easiest. But, with God's help, you can not only discern what is wise but receive the courage to act on it.

Perhaps now you're tying off at a port along the way to your destination, or perhaps you feel like you've

NOTES

reached your destination. You may be wondering what's next. Should you get off and find a new ship and crew? Should you restock, reorient, and head back out for open waters?

This is a big question that is deeply relational. Variations on that question might sound like: How long should our group meet together? When is it time to part ways? How do you know?

The questions above are natural and good questions, but they aren't the best questions. There are three questions that help leaders and groups determine the best way forward. It is best if these are routinely asked at the Route-Planning Session before each season of a group.

The first question is, **"Are we maturing and continuing to grow?"** It's remarkably easy to drift into just learning information and skipping the whole "live it out" part. Growth comes through applying what you're learning in the context of relationships. If the answer to this question is "no," then re-evaluate what kind of "ship" you're sailing and how you're spending your time together. Are you practicing that messy, spark-filled, iron sharpens iron part of relationships? Are you digging into how you can apply truth to your real, daily lives?

The second question is, **"Are we becoming more known by each other?"** If you remember back to the three levels of relationships on page 54, having level three relationships is hard work. And as such, it's easy to get stuck at level two. Heck, it's easy to go *back* to level two when things get sticky. If the answer to this question is "no," it may be a good time to re-examine your crew culture or group values and commitments. Where are you getting stuck? Is there a pattern happening that dissuades people from sharing?

Third and last, **"Are we overflowing and becoming more focused on others?"** God has designed each of us uniquely as parts of the Body, each with our own calling. If we are continuing to mature and grow (the first question), then we will inevitably become more focused on others. We will begin using more of our time, talents, and treasures to love and serve others, rather than focusing solely on our own needs. If the answer to this question is "no," then you may need to change your route or redesign your ship. Do you need to include more service opportunities? Would it help to set aside time to dream up ways to love others in your life?

If the answer to these three questions is "yes," then keep on going! If the answer is "no" to any or all of the questions, then evaluate why that is. You may need to go back to the drawing board of your goals as a group, or you may need to mix up your route and activities. It might be time to form different groups. Perhaps some of you are feeling called to start a group in your neighborhood in order to love those living in your proximity. Maybe some of you feel like you could be more vulnerable with and known by people in their own life stage (parents of preschoolers, empty-nesters, etc.). That's okay. Asking and honestly answering those three questions will help you evaluate where you want to go next. This kind of conversation takes courage and, depending on your group, could be difficult. Do your best to be honest, listen to understand each other, and give grace generously as you look and listen for what the Spirit is telling you.

If you've decided to continue together, then it's time to get into the nuts and bolts of the next season's route. Remember, this doesn't only mean looking at what kind of studies or curriculums you want to go through, it also means deciding how you'll pursue connection, relationships, service, and whatever else your group has chosen as a priority.

NOTES

ROUTE-PLANNING SESSION

Read as a group: Welcome back! Now is the time to re-evaluate your Group Map. We'll revisit the different parts of your group, guide you through the questions we introduced in the Diving Deeper section, and then help you plot your next route.

Connect

 **20% OF YOUR TIME (15-20 MINUTES)**

- Open in prayer.

- Warm up questions:

  » What is something God has been teaching you in this past season?

  » What is a personal area of growth you hope to experience in the next six months?

Learn

10% OF YOUR TIME

Have someone read the following prayer by navigator and explorer, Sir Francis Drake, before your jump into your route planning.

"Disturb us, Lord, when
We are too well pleased with ourselves,
When our dreams have come true
Because we have dreamed too little,
When we arrived safely
Because we sailed too close to the shore.

Disturb us, Lord, when
With the abundance of things we possess
We have lost our thirst
For the waters of life;
Having fallen in love with life,
We have ceased to dream of eternity
And in our efforts to build a new earth,
We have allowed our vision
Of the new Heaven to dim.

Disturb us, Lord, to dare more boldly,
To venture on wider seas
Where storms will show your mastery;
Where losing sight of land,
We shall find the stars.

We ask You to push back
The horizons of our hopes;
And to push into the future
In strength, courage, hope, and love."

NOTES

Live

 **70% OF YOUR TIME**

- Discuss the "big three" critical questions *(15-20 minutes):*

  » Are we maturing and continuing to grow?

  » Are we becoming more known by each other?

  » Are we overflowing and becoming more focused on others?

- Pull out last season's Group Map and revisit the Core Components of your group *(15-20 minutes):*

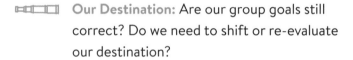 **Our Destination:** Are our group goals still correct? Do we need to shift or re-evaluate our destination?

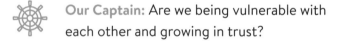 **Our Captain:** Are we being vulnerable with each other and growing in trust?

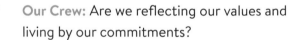 **Our Crew:** Are we reflecting our values and living by our commitments?

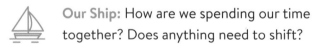 **Our Ship:** How are we spending our time together? Does anything need to shift?

PLAN THE ROUTE FOR THE NEXT SEASON!

(20-30 minutes)

It's not easy to plan ahead, and it's even harder to stick to it! Below we've included a calendar for you to brainstorm and choose your next four to six months together. Before you hammer out the details, get everyone's thoughts out on the table with the following questions. Refer to pages 93 and 94 for ideas.

- What are a few areas you would like to learn more about?

- What are a few areas you would like to grow in?

- What is an area of serving that you feel particularly drawn to? While we all can and should serve on our own, there is a uniquely powerful element to doing it together.

NOTES

- What are a few fun social activities you would like to do as a group?

 Tip: Consider doing an overnight retreat together once or twice a year. This can be a key element in the kind of groups people talk about for the rest of their lives. Is this something your group is interested in? How could you make it happen?

Narrow the Focus: Start looking for similarities in everyone's answers. Use the calendar on page 120 or print out calendars from *trueface.org/embark-group* and start actually putting things on your calendar. Remember, your calendar reflects your priorities, so if you haven't written it down, the odds of it really happening aren't good.

LAST AND CRITICAL STEP:

Put another Route-Planning Session on the calendar. This is a time to re-evaluate goals, check in on how everybody is doing, and do the same process of thinking through the next season's calendar and content plan.

	SUN	MON	TUES	WED	THUR	FRI	SAT

	SUN	MON	TUES	WED	THUR	FRI	SAT

SUN	MON	TUES	WED	THUR	FRI	SAT

SUN	MON	TUES	WED	THUR	FRI	SAT

SUN	MON	TUES	WED	THUR	FRI	SAT

SUN	MON	TUES	WED	THUR	FRI	SAT

Looking for your next group study?

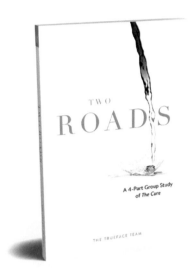

When many of us first met Jesus, we imagined a life full of authentic relationships, vibrant faith, and deep joy. But down the road, we find ourselves exhausted from trying to keep up, frustrated by our habitual issues, or just plain burnt out.

What if there was a different road?

A road that led to real, authentic community—the kind where the worst parts of you can be known, and you'll be loved more in the telling of it? What if that life of being authentically known and loved is real, and Jesus is inviting you to join Him in it?

Exploring the first three chapters of Trueface's flagship book, *The Cure*, through videos, discussion questions and scripture, *Two Roads* is designed to help your group travel beyond the mask and begin experiencing real, authentic relationships rooted in grace.

Get your copy at *trueface.org/the-cure*

ℳ TRUEFACE

Small Group Studies

TWO ROADS

Explore the first three chapters of *The Cure* in-depth with this small group study. *Two Roads* is designed to help your group travel beyond the mask and start experiencing real, authentic relationships through videos, discussion questions, scripture and application.

THE HEART OF MAN PARTICIPANT GUIDE

With contributions from Jackie Hill Perry, Dan Allender, WM Paul Young, Jay Stringer and John and Stasi Eldredge, this Trueface resource guides your group through unpacking and processing *The Heart of Man* movie and how to experience the love of the Father in the midst of our darkest struggles.

Books

THE CURE

Unpacking our view of ourselves and our view of God, *The Cure* invites you to remove your mask and experience God's lavish grace. This flagship book explores identity, community, sin, healing, destiny, and more as you discover that maybe God isn't who you think he is...and neither are you.

THE CURE FOR GROUPS

Do you want the kind of small group people will talk about the rest of their lives? A practical guide to starting (or re-igniting) your group, *The Cure for Groups* unpacks five Core Components to build a group that's bursting with life, depth, and the kind of life-changing community Jesus modeled for us.

THE CURE AND PARENTS

Travel with the Clawson family on their summer vacation as they struggle to navigate their family dynamics. Told partly through narrative and partly through teaching, this resource is for anyone wanting to bring grace to their family.

TRUST FOR TODAY

This 365-day devotional invites you to experience grace in your daily life, both in the big moments and the details of life. Use these short readings to incorporate grace into your everyday.

BO'S CAFÉ

Steven Kerner is living the dream in southern California, until his wife kicks him out after another angry outburst. Walk with Steven and his eccentric mentor Andy as they explore Steven's unresolved problems and performance-based life, rediscovering the restoration and healing only God's grace can provide.

THE ASCENT OF A LEADER

Become the leader people want to follow by opening yourself up to the influences that develop character: enduring relationships with friends, family and God. *The Ascent of a Leader* guides you through cultivating extraordinary character in your home, company, community, and every other arena of life.

BEHIND THE MASK

When sin enters our lives, we have automatic, God-given responses. If we are the one who sinned, our response is guilt. If we are sinned against, our response is hurt. Explore these two involuntary responses and how they can lead to painful patterns of hiding and hurting, unless we allow the grace of Jesus to heal us.

Robby Angle

Robby is the President and CEO of Trueface. He lives in Dawsonville, Georgia with his wife Emily and their eight children.

Prior to serving at Trueface, Robby served for over seven years at North Point Community Church in Atlanta, Georgia founded by Andy Stanley. In his role, Robby utilized Trueface resources through his positions as Director of Adult Ministry Environments and Director of Men's Groups.

Robby and Emily both worked as Licensed Professional Counselors, facilitating group therapy. Prior to joining North Point, they also served with with Samaritan's Purse in Pakistan and Myanmar overseeing international disaster response teams. Robby and Emily received a Masters in Community Counseling from Appalachian State University. Angle also holds a business degree from the University of Florida, and a Certificate in Biblical Studies from Dallas Theological Seminary.

He loves Trueface and the way it has created such a unique and effective way for teaching complex biblical principles of truth and grace and moving people from pleasing God to trusting God with their new identity.

TRUEFACE

beyond the mask